I0788147

Flying Like an Eagle

Juli Lubelczyk

For Peter

May your story help others fly.

-Mom

Acknowledgments

So many people have helped me bring this dream to life. Shout outs for my publication team: Paul, Ryan, and Emma. You have been a joy to work with, and I look forward to future projects together.

This book would not have been possible without the help of Gwena and Gerry Herman, coaches of the Bennett Blazers adaptive sports program at Kennedy Krieger. Peter's time with you was such a gift, giving him joy, belonging, confidence and purpose. It's this same impact that I want others to know is available. From this, the dream began. Thank you also for letting me come shadow during practices and games, for proofing the sports side of the story, and especially for believing in this mission.

Liz & Liz, Ann, Andrea, Kathy, you have prayed this dream to life. Cheri, your guidance gave me the courage to keep going. Thank you for being by my side every step of the way.

Finally, to my husband Jeff, your support means the world to me! Your belief in the story and in me as a writer started years ago when God initially gave me the idea. Your willingness to remember, your listening ear, your thoughtful questions and gentle suggestions were all so important in bringing this story to life. You heped make our time with Peter rich and full. Thank you for helping me bring him to life again in these pages.

And most importantly, I praise my Creator God. You gave me these words. You continue to lead me on this writing journey and in my daily life. May you be honored with this offering. - Juli

Table of Contents

Chapter 1

"Yes! I win again!" Peter called out, grinning at his best friend Justin. They were playing video games in Justin's basement.

"How many is that? 4 out of 5 games?" he asked.

"Yes," said Justin. "Now, can we please do something else? If you love this basketball game so much, let's go outside and shoot some real hoops. We'll see who wins this time!" he added as he put down his controller.

Ugh! Thought Peter. *Video games are so much easier.*

As he watched Justin shut down the game system, he thought back to PE earlier that week. They were working on basketball skills. He hated it. It was hard to keep his balance while he tried to shoot, and the dribbling drills were just plain embarrassing since he had to hold on to something to keep himself steady while he walked. Still, PE was better than any other class at school. He loved sports. He loved to win. He loved racing and going fast and being first.

But that seemed to be happening less and less unless it was during video games. Since the end of first grade, he had become increasingly unsteady. He could stand up and walk, even jog a little. The problem was keeping his balance. Ever since he'd gotten sick, he'd needed a wall to hold onto while walking or even another person. It wasn't that big a deal when he was little. But now he was in third grade and he used a walker to get around. He could no longer play baseball, running was a joke, and now shooting hoops with his best friend was getting more and more frustrating.

Still, he got up and headed out the patio door with Justin, holding onto the couch and then the wall, as he made his way outside. He found a good spot leaning against the half wall near the side of the court to steady himself.

Justin bounced the ball a few times before stepping up to the foul line. Lining up his feet, he dribbled the ball twice, squared up his elbow, and flicked his wrist at the end. The ball sailed with a perfect arc and swooshed through the net.

"Great shot," Peter said as Justin ran after the ball. Peter caught the bounce pass for a turn. It was hard at this angle as he couldn't use the backboard. Still, he dribbled a few times, and then paused a moment to steady himself while picking up the ball to shoot. Keeping his legs pressed firmly against the wall, he lined up the shot and tried to imitate Justin's release. The ball left his hands with a decent arc but it was way short – didn't even touch the rim or the net.

"Air ball!!" sang Justin, laughing as he ran after the ball.

"I'm just getting warmed up," Peter laughed sheepishly. "Pass it back and let me try again."

"Uh-huh. Sure." Justin smirked as he passed the ball back to Peter.

Peter steadied himself against the wall again as he caught the ball and bounced it once. He lined up his shot and thought about what his PE teacher had said about using his legs to add strength to a shot. It was really hard to bend his knees and stay steady, but with the back of his feet on the wall, he bent his knees as far as he could without losing his balance – which wasn't much – and stood as he raised his arms and flicked the ball out of his hand. This shot was higher and went farther, but it just bumped the rim as it was still too low.

"Hey, that was way better than last shot," Justin called as he chased after the ball. Scooping it up, Justin turned and dribbled the ball down the right side of the lane. Several feet from the basket, he picked up the ball and made an easy lay-up.

Back and forth they took turns - Justin making almost every basket, Peter trying to get the ball near the rim After his third air ball, he was about ready to give up.

"No man, you got this," Justin called as he chased the ball down and passed it back to Peter. Peter dribbled once, again steadying himself against the wall. Then he stood, squaring up his elbow, and bent his knees. But instead of releasing the ball, he felt himself start to fall to the right. Thankfully, he got his hands down to catch himself before he hit his head.

"Hey, you ok?" asked Justin. "Do you want me to get your walker so you can sit on the seat to shoot?"

"No, I'm good," Peter said. "Just let me get back up."

They were both used to this, unfortunately. But as Peter pressed his legs against the wall again to steady himself, he remembered Tim laughing at him during PE this week when he'd fallen at school. Instead of lining up his shot, he took the ball with both hands over his head and slammed it into the ground. Looking like a bounce pass but with way more force, the ball bounced hard on the ground about half way between Peter and the basket. Then it shot up high and fast, arcing beautifully into the basket.

"Woosh!" shouted Justin. "Look at that! Nothing but net! Man, let me try that."

Peter laughed and Justin sprinted over. They spent the rest of the hour, making up trick shots. Bouncing the ball to make a shot, Peter bounced the ball to Justin on the run for a lay-up or jump shot, even both of them sitting on the ground around the court shooting the ball without using their legs or lower bodies. Sounds of laughter filled the court until finally, Justin plopped down on the ground next to Peter.

"Whew! I'm pooped!" he said, wiping his forehead.

"You got quite a workout chasing the balls," Peter said. "Man! That one play, the bounce pass to you at the foul line, that was a sweet shot. You were like three feet off the ground."

Justin laughed. "I doubt I was that high, dude. That's like as tall as you," he joked.

"Hey, I'm not that short!"

"Well, you better work on those estimation skills, Pete! But, yeah, that was a great play. Let's go get something to drink."

He stood up and grabbed Peter's hand. Pulling him up, Justin gave Peter a minute to steady himself. Then holding onto his best friend, Peter walked with him into the house.

That night, after dinner and some TV, his mom switched off the television. Peter climbed upstairs and got himself ready for bed. As he crawled into bed, he was surprised when both his mom and dad came into the room to tell him goodnight.

Instead of leaning down to give him a kiss, his mom sat on the end of his bed and his dad sat down at his desk. Peter looked back and forth at each of them.

"Pete, there's something we want you to think about," his dad began. "We've been talking with Dr. Santos, and she thinks it might be time to start using a wheelchair."

"What?" Peter exclaimed.

"A wheelchair, Peter. Remember when we went to Disney World last year? You used a wheelchair in the park so you didn't have to walk all the time. It kept you from getting too tired, and we had a blast running around the park, going from ride to ride. Remember?"

"Yeah, I remember. That was kinda cool. But do you mean like all the time? I can still walk. Why do I need a wheelchair?"

"Well, you are getting older and taller Peter," his mom replied. "You just were complaining the other day about falling in PE. I know you don't like using your walker at times. It adds time to lock or unlock the brakes and slows you down. Also, it's important to save up your energy to help you make it through the day. When you are more tired, you are more at risk for falls or worse."

"You could actually do more things on your own with a wheelchair than with a walker," Peter's Dad chimed in. "Now that you're getting older, it might be a better option. Just think about it. We can talk more about it tomorrow."

After a kiss from each, they flipped off the light. Rusty, Peter's Shitzu, came into the room as his parents walked out. As he came up to the bed, Peter scooped him up and set him on his chest.

"Hey, Rusty," he said as he stroked his dog. Rusty licked his nose and then plopped down on the bed beside him. He curled up against Peter's side as Peter kept petting his head.

A wheelchair? Peter thought.

Chapter 2

Peter woke up in a bright room. The light around the blinds gave evidence of a sunny day. He hadn't slept well. He kept thinking about what his parents had said last night.

What would it be like to use a wheelchair all the time? Would his friends think it was cool or weird? He knew his walker was annoying, but how would he play basketball? What did his dad mean he could do more things by himself? At least now he could leave his walker at times if there was something else he could hold on to. A wheelchair would always be there.

His thoughts continued to spin as he got dressed and scooted downstairs. Sliding down the carpeted steps was faster and more fun than walking.

As he sat down to breakfast, his mom joined him and his dad at the table. She set down her coffee.

"Peter, later we are going to head up to a sports program we want you to see," she started. "Today, they have a swimming session and basketball practice. We thought you might enjoy meeting some of these athletes."

"Do I get to swim and play too?" Peter asked with his mouth full of cereal.

"Don't talk with your mouth full, Peter! That's gross," his mom said.

"No play time today, Pete. We'll just be watching. I think you'll be impressed though," his dad replied.

Watching? Peter thought. Sure whatever. Hopefully, it wouldn't take all day. He really wanted to get to the next level on his new video game this weekend.

His mom had said it would take about a half hour to get there. They had to drive into the city as the gym was in the north part of Easton. Staring out the window, his mind immediately went back to his parents' suggestion of moving into a wheelchair. Why couldn't his life be like all of his friends?

His classmates were great when he first got sick. They all made cards for him while he was in the hospital. Everyone was so excited when he came back to school. Even people he didn't play with at recess wanted to sit with him at lunch. Everyone wanted to help carry his things. It didn't last long, of course, but it was kind of exciting.

He remembered when his mom came in to explain to the class what mitochondrial (my-toe-con-dree-ul) disease was. She told them how our bodies are made up of really small parts called cells. Inside the cells, the mitochondria make energy for our bodies: energy for things we don't think about like breathing, digesting food, and our heart beating, but also energy to move and think and learn… energy for everything. My body had trouble making that energy correctly and, when there wasn't enough energy, things could happen.

She said a body with mito was like a remote-control car. She asked the class to picture an RC car, turning, speeding, going all over the place. But then, when the batteries start to wear down, the car starts to go slower. It doesn't turn as well, and then maybe can't turn at all. It only goes straight. Then, you can turn the car on but it won't go far, and one day won't go at all. You can rev it, but it won't move.

She said the mitochondria are the batteries in our bodies. When we eat good food and get enough sleep, we recharge our batteries and keep our bodies running great, able to grow and learn and play. But with mito disease, recharging the batteries is harder. Because the mitochondria don't make energy right in the first place, it's easy to run out of energy quicker. So different parts of the body can have trouble doing what they are supposed to. Like an RC car, eventually, things are harder to do, and over time, a person with mito can no longer do what they could before. That's why I now have trouble keeping my balance. Wherever the breakdown happens in making energy decides what parts of the body will have trouble. So different people with mito can have different problems.

Mito isn't contagious, she told them. You can't catch it from another person - It's something you are born with. She told them about the special vitamins I take to help my body make energy better. Scientists and doctors were working hard to learn how to help people with mito, she had said. But right now, it wasn't something we could fix. We had to do what we could to save up energy and that included finding new ways to do some things, like using a walker to help me get around school.

A boy walking his dog on the sidewalk as they stopped at a stoplight caught Peter's eye. It was the same kind of dog as Rusty, but it had black spots instead of brown. His mind shifted back to the wheelchair. Did this mean he was getting worse? Did his parents think he wasn't going to be able to walk soon?

His stomach started to feel funny and his muscles tightened up a little in his arms. He took a deep breath to try to calm down.

"Here we are," his Mom called out. "Welcome to the home of the Easton Eagles!"

"Hey, they use the same mascot as the Philadelphia Eagles," Peter said smiling, as he thought of his favorite football team. "These guys are lucky! I should have worn one of my Eagles shirts."

Grabbing onto his walker which his Dad had gotten out of the trunk, Peter climbed out of the car and looked around. There were only a few cars in the parking lot. But as he walked toward the building, he noticed every single handicap spot was full. *That's weird,* he thought.

"Don't go too fast on this hill," his mom warned. They were headed to a door around the back where they were supposed to meet Coach Mike. "I'm fine, Mom" Peter grumbled back. She was always telling him to slow down, be careful, watch out for this or that. He knew she just wanted to keep him safe, but it made him feel like a baby. Other kids fell down and scraped their knees. Why was it such a big deal if he did too?

As they stepped inside the building, Peter found himself in a huge gym. It had six basketball hoops. One on each end made a full-size court. But there were also two baskets on each side across from each other. He saw there were curtain dividers that could be pulled to separate the gym into smaller courts. That's cool, he thought.

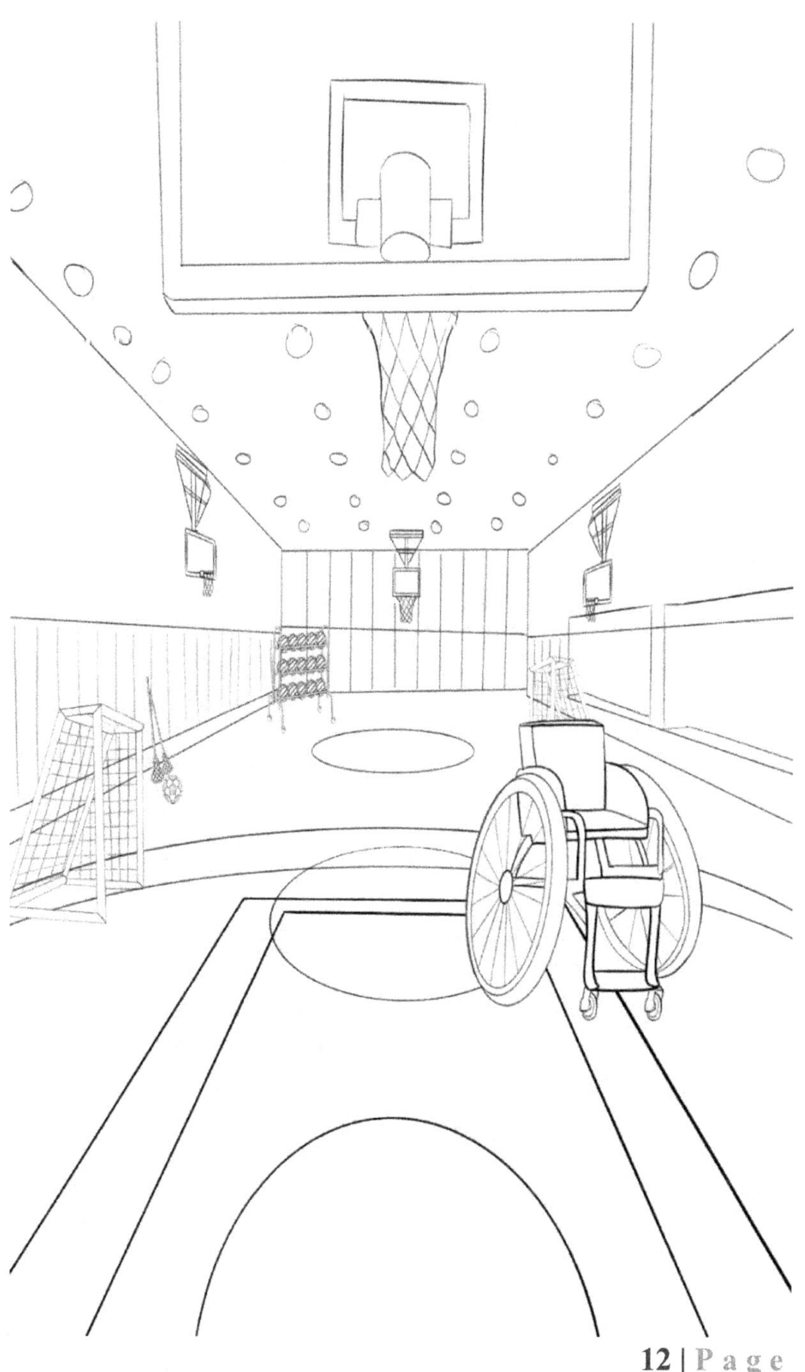

Then he noticed green lanes on the floor. A track! The gym had a track of three lanes that circled all the way around the courts. Along the walls, he saw bins of sports equipment: balls, lacrosse sticks, bowling pins. There was a disc golf basket in one corner and a couple of soccer goals stacked on top of each other. Stacks of blue mats like they had at school were also scattered around the edge of the gym. This place looks pretty fun!

Peter shook hands with Coach Mike when he arrived. He had a giant mustache over a big smile. His eyes crinkled when he smiled. He was tall like his dad but more muscular. He looked like an athlete.

"Welcome to the Eagles, Peter," Coach Mike said.

"Thank you," Peter replied. "You've got a lot of sports stuff in here. It looks like our gym at school but way bigger."

"Yes, we do every sport you can think of here at Easton: soccer, volleyball, tennis, baseball, basketball of course, but also bowling, bocci, track, even hockey. If it's a sport, we can make it happen."

"That's cool. Mom said you have swim and basketball practice today? Do you have a team that competes?"

"We sure do! The swim team finished Nationals a bit ago so this is more for staying in shape and teaching new swimmers. Almost all of our kids compete in at least one event. This gives us time to find the best event for each athlete.

We are now in basketball season," Coach Mike continued. "We have several teams based on ages and skill levels. We are hosting a big tournament President's Day weekend. So practice can get a little intense.

You should come back for the tournament!" Coach Mike added.

"Let's head over to the pool. That's where Coach Jenny and the kids are. She's my wife. We used to run a program up in Boston, but then we moved down here while our kids are in college."

Peter headed through the locker room with his dad and Coach Mike. He noticed how smooth everything was. Often as he went through doors, his walker would get stuck on ridges in the doorway. Here he had no trouble getting his walker through doorways and around benches. Everything was spaced out great. He was surprised at what a difference it made.

Peter could smell the chlorine as they moved out of the locker room. His mom joined them as she'd come through the girl's side.

As they walked up to the pool, he could see splashes in the lanes where the kids were swimming. He saw a woman in the pool about halfway down with a whistle. That must be Coach Jenny, he thought.

Just then a swimmer reached the end of the pool in front of them. She put her arms on the edge of the pool and pushed her body up out of the water. As she did, she flipped around to sit down on the edge.

Peter felt himself stare. She had no legs.

Chapter 3

"How can she do that?" Peter whispered.

Thankfully, she didn't notice him. He couldn't help but stare.

She had red hair sticking out of her white swimcap. She wore a black one-piece swimsuit and bright orange goggles. From the back, she looked like any regular person. But from this angle, Peter could see her legs and they were not there! Her right leg stopped just below the knee. Her left leg was shorter. It didn't have a knee.

How can you swim with no legs? Peter wondered.

He watched as the girl fixed her goggles and slipped back into the pool. In the water, she looked like a regular swimmer. She was on her back this time. Her arms rotated in and out of the water and you saw splashes following her as she kicked. Peter realized she kicked her legs just like he did. They just weren't as long as his.

Finally, Peter broke his gaze from the girl and looked around the pool. Several parents were sitting on benches along the wall. Everyone seemed to have a wheelchair beside them. Two had walkers like his and one had what looked like crutches leaning against the bench. But most of the parents were next to wheelchairs.

While his parents talked with Coach Mike, Peter started watching the other swimmers. The lanes closest to them were filled with swimmers doing different kinds of strokes. One lane had several older kids doing butterfly. The muscles in their arms looked like a grown-up. He watched as their bodies bent back and forth with their kicks. The next lane was backstroke. The red-haired girl was in that group. Next to them was a lane for freestyle. Those kids looked younger and Coach Jenny was in that lane. Every once in a while, she would walk beside the swimmer, sometimes putting her hand under their belly to help them stay up.

Two sharp whistle blasts caught everyone's attention.

"Ten more minutes" Coach Jenny called to the bigger kids. "You guys with me, swim to the edge. Let's start getting you out of the pool."

As the five young swimmers swam to the edge, several parents came forward with towels and wheelchairs. Coach Jenny lifted each swimmer onto the edge. Moms and Dads wrapped each child in a towel, collecting their goggles and swim caps.

None of the kids had missing legs like the red-haired girl. But once dried off a bit, each child climbed or was lifted into a wheelchair. One of the biggest kids had climbed into his chair by himself and headed over.

"Hi," the boy called. "I'm Juan. Are you joining the Eagles?" he asked as he rolled his wheelchair up to Peter.

"Joining? Um, I don't think so. I don't know. My mom and dad just said we were coming to watch today. I'm Peter," he replied.

"Well, you should join. The Eagles are the best! I've been coming since I was in Kindergarten. Now I'm in second grade. So that means it's been over two years. I swam the 50-meters freestyle at Nationals. I only got a ribbon though. I'm still learning to swim fast. But I'm better at basketball. As long as

I use the low basket. But I'm awesome at hockey! That's totally my favorite!"

Juan paused to take a breath. The whole time he talked he was rolling his chair back and forth. He had a lot of energy.

"Hockey?" Peter asked. "How can you play hockey if you can't walk?"

"We use a sled. I sit on one end and it has a long blade under it like an ice skate. Our hockey sticks are shorter since we are sitting. We use our sticks to help us skate around. It's the totally best game in the whole world!

"I like your walker," he continued. "I have one too, but it's red. I still use it sometimes at school. But here at Easton, I use the wheelchair for most of my sports."

"I'm sorry. I didn't know you could walk. I noticed there were lots of chairs by the pool. Does everyone here use a wheelchair?" Peter asked.

"Well, how can you play wheelchair basketball without a wheelchair?" Juan laughed.

"No, I mean like all the time," Peter said.

Just then Coach Jenny walked up. "Juan, you need to get to the locker room. Get changed for basketball and leave Peter alone. I'm sure you're talking his ear off," she smiled.

"Hi, Peter. I'm Coach Jenny. Welcome to the Eagles. I heard your question. Not everyone here uses a wheelchair, but many do. Some have walkers like yours, and Stephen often uses his crutches. It depends on what they need to move."

"I didn't know the Eagles weren't for regular kids," Peter said. "My folks just said we were coming to watch some athletes today."

"Regular kids? Didn't Juan seem regular to you?" she asked.

Peter felt his cheeks get hot. "Yes, ma'am."

Coach Jenny started laughing. "Relax Peter. I'm just giving you a hard time. We like to tease and laugh and have fun here at Easton. You're right. The Easton Eagles are for athletes who need some type of adaptive equipment to play a sport: a wheelchair to play basketball or race, a sled to play hockey. But know that our kids are regular kids in every way but one. Whatever the reason they need adaptive equipment makes them special not different - special because they find a way to play instead of letting their challenge stop them.

Come on, let's head to the court. You'll see what I mean."

"What do you think, Peter?" his Dad asked as they made their way back through the locker room to the gym.

"Why didn't you tell me?" Peter snapped. "I felt so stupid talking to Coach Jenny!"

"I'm sorry, Peter," his Dad said. "Mom and I thought it would be a neat surprise for you. We didn't want you to think anything one way or another, but just be open to watching these kids play. We didn't mean to make you feel embarrassed."

Peter pushed himself ahead of his dad once they reached the gym. He couldn't help but feel a little tricked.

Just then, Juan sped past. "Hi, Peter!"

Juan made his chair curve toward the basket with one hand, holding a basketball in the other. As he neared the basket, he used both hands to shoot the ball. It swooshed through the net.

"Oh yeah! That's right," Juan cheered for himself.

Coach Mike blew a whistle and all of the older kids gathered around him at one end of the gym. The other kids rolled down to the other end where Coach Jenny sat in a wheelchair.

Peter noticed that these chairs were different than the ones the kids had climbed into by the pool. The seat had low sides or none at all, and a small back instead of the high back, armrests and push handles he had seen on the others. All of the kids had what looked like a seatbelt across their legs, strapping them into the chair. A few had straps for their feet too.

"On the red line," Coach Jenny called.

As each player moved into place, Coach Jenny bounced a ball to each kid. Only two kids missed catching the ball and had to roll away to chase it.

"Remember," Coach Jenny said. "No more than two pushes between dribbles. Turn at half-court. Go"

Each player took off in their chair. After two pushes, they would dribble the ball beside their chair. One kid bounced their ball off the base of the wheel. As he wheeled after it, Peter realized the wheels slanted in at the top, wider at the base.

The red-haired girl was in this group too. She had what looked like socks on the end of her legs. She quickly did two strong pushes using both hands while the ball sat in her lap. Then she dribbled the ball once or twice as her chair started to slow down. She put the ball back in her lap and pushed again. *She's really good*, Peter thought.

He sat on the seat of his walker in the middle of the gym, near the door to the locker room. He turned to see what Coach Mike was doing with the older kids.

They all were lined up facing the wall. Each athlete had a basketball and they were bouncing the ball above their heads against the wall. From where he was, he couldn't tell if they were holding the ball so they could shoot it or pass it. But he knew all that over-the-head work would make his arms tired. And they had just finished swimming!

Peter was still a little mad at his parents for not telling him what to expect. But he had to admit these athletes were really cool. Could he maybe join the Eagles? If so, maybe using a wheelchair wouldn't be so bad.

Chapter 4

"No legs? No way!" Justin exclaimed.

They were eating lunch in the cafeteria and Peter was telling him about his visit to the Easton Eagles sports program.

"Yes way! I couldn't believe it. You'd never know watching her in the water. All of the kids looked like any other kid in the water. It wasn't until they got out that you noticed they couldn't walk. Well, some could walk. There were some with walkers like mine and one kid used crutches. Some could even use the wall to stand up and move into their wheelchair themselves.

I was really happy to see that! I thought using a wheelchair meant you couldn't walk at all. I don't want people thinking that about me when I get mine."

"What?" Justin yelled. "You're getting a wheelchair?!!"

"Not so loud, Justin," Peter replied. Oops! He hadn't meant to let that cat out of the bag.

"I might. It's not for sure. My parents are talking about it.

Please don't say anything. I don't want to talk about it here. People can hear us. I'll fill you in when we get to your place after school."

That afternoon, Peter's mom dropped Peter off at Justin's to hang out while she ran some errands.

"You've got your homework done, right?" she asked.

"Yes, Mom. Everything's finished. So no need to rush back, ok? Justin and I want to try out a new strategy for his video game.

"Hi, Mrs. Russo," Peter said as he pushed his walker through the door she held open. She waved at his mom as she backed out of the drive way.

"Justin's downstairs in the basement. He already took down some snacks and drinks. Help yourself," she said.

"Thanks, Mrs. Russo!" Peter called out as he slid down the steps. He left his walker parked by the basement door.

"Hey, Pete!" Justin called out as Peter scooted across the floor to the couch. "Mom bought Cheetos!"

"Alright! My favorite," Peter cheered as he grabbed a handful.

The boys quickly settled into the game, discussing strategy. They took turns, learning from each other's mistakes and soon had mastered the level that had stumped them for a week.

After a bit, they took a break to eat some more Cheetos and drink some Gatorade.

"So, tell me about your wheelchair! When are you getting it? You can do a wheelie in the hallway at school!" Justin rattled on.

"Good grief," Peter laughed. "You sound like this is a good thing!"

Justin looked up. "Don't you?" he asked.

"I don't know," Peter replied. "I mean, it would be fun to ride around and go crazy down the hall. But what will the kids think? Will they laugh? Will they think I'm stupid because I use a chair?

I have to admit, I was shocked to see how normal all the kids were at the gym this weekend. I guess I thought if they couldn't walk, they'd be weird or something. I don't know why. But it just really surprised me that they were just like me. They were talking about what level they were on in Mario Kart. One kid was complaining about having to go home and do math homework. Everyone was grumping at their folks for making them wear coats when we left. It was just like being with all the kids at school.

Yet, here I am, a kid with a walker myself, thinking they're different, or not normal, or maybe dumb. I was the dumb one," he paused.

"But I can totally hear Tim coming up with another reason to make fun of me if I'm in a wheelchair. 'Watch out everyone! Here comes the domino. Won't take him long to crash that chair I bet… We can call him Pile Up Peter…' or something stupid like that."

"Forget about Tim," Justin replied. "He's just trying to make people not notice how weird he is! No one listens to him or believes anything he says.

What I don't understand is why your parents want you to get a wheelchair when you can walk. You're zipping all over the place with your walker."

"I know. That was my first question too. But Mom explained my body uses more energy to stand and walk than it would need to sit and push myself around. Dr. Santos says it's better for my body to use less energy because then all the energy I have will last longer.

When I get home from school, I have to lay down most days for a while. That's why I can never just come home from school with you. If I don't get some rest or if I keep going until my energy is used up, it's more likely I can get sick or have a dangerous fall or even a seizure. I have to do what I can to avoid another energy crash like I had last year. That's what put me in the hospital," Peter explained.

"Well, you don't want that to happen again, that's for sure!" Justin said. "And think about all the cool stuff you could do in a chair. Wheelies! Racing in the hallway! Hey, you can give me a ride to class!"

"No way man! You are way too heavy," Peter laughed. "I don't want your butt in my lap.

But it sure would make basketball more fun. And Coach Mike said they could make any sport happen for any kid! Maybe I could play baseball again! I don't know how track works when you can't run. But I think you can race in a chair. I miss running soooo much. I bet I could kick butt in a wheelchair."

"Yeah, man!" Justin agreed. "Remember your Dad told you that you'd be able to do more stuff by yourself in a wheelchair? Did he just mean sports? What else did he mean?"

"I don't know," Peter answered. "I wouldn't be able to go up or down stairs in a chair. I guess I'd still have to get out to climb up or slide down. But then how would my chair get to me?"

"But you don't take your walker upstairs now, do you? Don't you just crawl up the stairs and scoot across the floor when you go up to your room?" Justin asked.

"That's true," Peter replied. "I don't know. It feels like it would change everything, but maybe it wouldn't. Mom and Dad said I could go up to Easton again this weekend and try out a chair. Juan said he uses his walker at home and for school. He just uses the wheelchair at Easton when he's doing his sports. Maybe I can be like that. Maybe I don't have to have it all the time.

If I didn't have to worry about falling over, I bet basketball would be way easier," Peter said.

"And way more fun!" Justin agreed.

Chapter 5

"Now loop that strap through the buckle and pull it tight but not so tight it hurts. It should be snug to keep you in the chair, but still allow you to move without rubbing on your legs," Coach Jenny explained as she helped Peter get into his assigned wheelchair.

"We'll start with this chair and see how it works for you. But we have others if this one doesn't feel right."

Peter looked down at the chair, noticing the slant of the wheels. He had joined the Easton Eagles and this was his first practice. He studied the chair, noticing many aspects designed to protect him. The slanted wheels should keep his hands safe since he pushed the chair at the top of the wheels. A bar crossed the front of the chair in front of his foot rest. That would protect his feet and legs from banging into other chairs as he moved around other players.

The seat back was fairly low and he could feel the chair tip a bit as he leaned back. He quickly leaned forward.

"Yes, it will feel a little like you're falling at times, Peter. But you'll get used to that. Realize it's almost impossible for you to tip over backwards. See this little wheel back here?" Coach Jenny asked.

Peter twisted in his chair and saw a bar across the back, like the one at his feet on the front. It had another bar reach from the center down to the floor with a small wheel at the end. When he looked out on the court at the other players, he saw it on the back of their chairs too.

"This little wheel will catch you and keep you from falling backwards," she explained. "It doesn't mean you can't flip your chair over. It does happen. But it takes a really big force to do so. Most chairs flip because players lean too far sideways to reach a ball. I don't think I've ever seen a kid fall backwards. Just take it easy today. You'll get used to the feel in no time. Your focus today needs to be on moving your chair."

Over the next half hour or so, Coach Jenny stayed near Peter explaining things but also letting him find things out on his own. He realized pushing with two hands at the same time made him go much faster, which he loved. It was like running again! Using one hand made his chair turn slightly in that direction. But if he grabbed one wheel and held it, he could make a sharp turn in that direction. Pushing the wheels backwards obviously made him go backwards. It really wasn't that hard once you got the hang of it.

In this first part of practice, everyone was playing together. The coaches had sent three kids to the middle of the court. Everyone else was lined up on one end. When the whistle blew, they had to race across the court to the other end without getting tagged. Once tagged, those players joined the others in the middle and helped tag others on the next round.

Being new and slow, Peter was tagged the first round most of the time, but it was fun. Whether trying not to get tagged or racing to tag others, he was moving. He wasn't falling over. Soon, he wasn't even the slowest one on the court since the little kids were playing too.

Coach Mike had explained that this practice time was for younger kids, called Junior Prep. At Easton, they divided the Prep kids into three groups. Competitive Prep players were usually 10-13 years or middle school kids. Peter's group would be 7-9 year olds and there was also a younger group. They would all work together on some drills but divide into groups most of the time. This opening game of tag was to get everyone warmed up and loose for the serious drills.

As the whistle blew, Peter focused on Juan. As soon as he saw Peter come in the door that afternoon, he'd raced over to say hi. He chatted non-stop about how excited he was Peter was joining the Eagles, and then shared all about the game they'd won last weekend. Now, Peter was determined to tag him.

Peter watched as Kolby raced up to Juan. She was just reaching out to tag him when Juan took advantage of her hands being off the wheel and he spun right. He looked back laughing as he raced forward. That's when Peter made his move. Instead of staying still and waiting for Juan to come, Peter started rolling toward the end of the court like he was a racer, not a tagger. Soon Juan caught up to him and Peter reached out as he went by.

"Gotcha!" Peter shouted.

"What? No way! Aw man," Juan cried as he slowed. "I thought you were a racer too, not a tagger."

They both laughed as they rolled back to the middle of the court for the next round.

The next drill was a bounce pass/shoot combination. Coach Mike took the younger kids center court and the other two groups each took one end. Now using the side baskets, which Peter realized were lower than the official ones on the ends of the gym, they had three courts, one for each group.

Coach Jenny was with his group and he saw a parent helping with the middle schoolers. They looked like they were playing a game.

"Peter, pay attention. Go join the line behind Juan," Coach Jenny called. Two lines had formed on either side of the basket. Coach Jenny and a few high school Eagles were lined up under the basket. They had come early for their practice which followed this one and joined in to help.

The first person in each line rolled out together. Juan had the ball and bounce-passed it to Coach Jenny in the middle. She then bounce-passed it to Kolby, the first person on her other side. Kolby caught the ball, did a push, then bounced it back. The three kept bouncing it between them in turn until they reached the other basket. Juan, who had the ball last, rolled up to the basket and made the shot. Then they all got in line under that basket.

Peter's group started out once Juan's group reached the first foul line. DeVonte had the ball and bounce passed it to Kevin, the high schooler in the middle. Kevin waited until Peter gave a big push and then softly bounce-passed it right into his lap. Peter caught the ball with both hands. As he leaned down with his push, his chest pushed the ball off his lap. "Shoot!"

"That's okay," Kevin called as he rolled over to pick it up. He held the ball against the bottom of his wheel. As the wheel rolled, it rolled the ball up into his hands.

That was cool, Peter thought.

"Try to use just your arms to push, Pete, when you have the ball. If you lean forward too much when you push, you'll lose the ball every time," Kevin explained.

"Okay," Peter called back. "Sorry about that," he called to DeVonte as they got back in line.

"Hey, it's only your first day," he called back. "My first day I couldn't even get my chair to turn," he laughed.

The next round went better. Peter caught the ball and pushed without losing it. He somehow managed to get the ball back to Kevin and DeVonte took his turn. They were almost to the basket when Peter's bounce pass was too close to Kevin's wheel. Thankfully he still caught it.

"Keep the pass in the middle between us," Kevin called out. He bounced the ball to DeVonte who made the layup.

Two more rounds and Peter was wiped! His arms felt like jelly and his hands were starting to hurt from pushing on the chair.

"Water break!" Coach Jenny called. Everyone rolled over to their parents and got a drink.

"So, what do you think?" Coach Jenny asked as she rolled up to Peter and his folks.

"It's awesome!" Peter exclaimed! "I love being able to play but my arms are like spaghetti."

"Yes, it will take a while for you to build up your strength. Your upper body gets quite a workout using a chair. You'll likely feel a little sore tomorrow. How are your hands? Do you have blisters yet? I can get you some gloves like Samson wears."

She looked at Peter's hands and his Mom rushed over.

"I'm fine, Mom," Peter huffed.

"Maybe you should sit out a bit, Peter," his Mom said.

"He actually has some calluses built up, Mrs. Thomas, probably from using his walker. But I'll go grab a pair of gloves he can use for the rest of practice," Coach Jenny said.

"Mom, I'm fine. I just need a drink."

"Alright, Peter. But be careful. It's okay if you need to sit out. You don't want to do too much and make yourself sick," his mom replied.

Peter didn't even bother answering. He rolled out onto the court, glad he had a way to be on his own. His mom was always so worried he might get sick again. Peter certainly didn't want to go back to the hospital, but he also wanted to live, to play, to have a life. If only she wouldn't hover so much and just let him be. *At least now he could escape to the court*, he thought grinning as he rejoined Juan.

After a few more drills, Coach Jenny put them in a three-on-three match. Peter was on Juan's team this time. Coach Jenny stayed with him the whole time. She started explaining some of the techniques for offense and defense. She showed him how to use his chair to block the path to the basket when the other team brought the ball down the court. By waiting on the front corner of the key, he could roll his chair to stay between the guard and the basket, forcing them wide so they couldn't shoot and had to pass. With his hands up, he could make it hard for them to see and pass.

On offense, the goal was to look down the court as you neared the three-point line. If you didn't have a path to the basket, the other players should triangle out from you so you could pass to one of them. Bounce passes were best as they were easier to catch. Sometimes, one of your teammates could be waiting down by the basket and make an easy jump shot off the backboard if you could get them the ball.

But it was hard! Peter started rolling his chair bent over with his chin on the ball. It kept rolling off his lap if he didn't. He thought Coach Jenny had him bring the ball down so often because it was the safest way for him to handle the ball. His arms were so tired his bounce passes weren't getting to the other players very well. The other team was getting lots of steals.

And there was so much to remember! You could only take two pushes before you had to dribble the ball. He had to make sure he dribbled the ball in front. He'd tried to dribble it beside his chair but it just hit his wheel and rolled out of bounds. He'd forgotten the wheels slanted out. You also had to always be looking for your teammates. If he waited to find them once he got stuck, the defense would try to take the ball from his lap or right out of his hands! His arms were so tired, it was hard to hold onto the ball.

Practice ended with train relays. Coach Jenny assigned lead rollers; thankfully the older athletes. Then she'd tell different kids to grab onto the handles on the back of their chairs. She had Peter join a train right away. Soon another kid had hold of his chair as he held onto Samson's chair. By the end, Samson was pulling 5 additional chairs!

Peter had had way too much fun to be upset at how bad he played. He waved goodbye to Juan as he headed back to his parents. Coach Jenny walked over to join them as he got out of the chair.

"Great job today, Peter! So glad you've joined the Eagles," she said.

"Didn't feel like a good job," Peter laughed. "I think I made more people chase balls today than catch them. I'm pretty bad at this."

"Don't say that, Peter. Repeat after me… I'm not bad at it," she started.

"I'm not bad at it," Peter repeated.

"I'm just new at it," Coach Jenny finished.

"I'm just new at it…. I'm not bad at wheelchair basketball, I'm just new at it," Peter stated. "I like that!"

"And it's true," Peter's Dad said as he wrapped his arm across his shoulders. "You looked like you had fun today. I'm really proud of you!"

"I'm proud of me too," Peter replied, with a grin from ear to ear.

Chapter 6

Peter woke up with the alarm after a restless night. Today was the first day taking his wheelchair to school. Once he'd agreed to use a wheelchair, everything moved so fast. He got fitted for the chair and that arrived in six weeks. During that time his parents decided to trade in his Mom's car for a van. It had a ramp that allowed Peter to roll right into the middle of the van and lock his chair in place. He could still ride in his Dads SUV and put the walker in the back if he was only going to be out for a short time. But now, the van would allow him to use his wheelchair most of the time.

He wasn't sure how he felt about using his chair at school. It was different than the chair he used for basketball. It had a higher back, arm rests, and handles where someone could push him. There was a head rest and foot rests. It had a tip bar just like his basketball chair so he couldn't flip it backwards. Many kids at Easton had similar chairs in bright colors – blues, greens, even hot pink. But Peter had chosen all black. It reminded him of his favorite sports car in a racing video game he loved. He was trying to convince his folks to add flames on the sides. So far, they'd said no. But he wasn't done trying.

His mind shifted to Easton. Basketball was going great. He wasn't the best player by far, but he'd finally scored a basket in their last practice. He was best at defense. He could tell where players were headed and block them every time. He was also getting good at grabbing the ball or knocking it away from players. The offense was still a bit tough though. He was getting stronger and could play longer. But he still struggled to not lose the ball when he was rolling and dribbling. His passes were getting better though.

He'd had to miss a week when he caught the flu. He'd had to go to the hospital and get an IV since he kept throwing up. It was dangerous for kids with mito to not eat, so whenever he got sick, he often had to go to the hospital to be safe. Now that he'd been there a few times, the staff knew him and his mom. It was becoming routine. Luckily, he was able to go home the next day. Still, he hated to miss any chance to play. Playing basketball was one thing he could do all by himself with no help from anyone. That's what made him agree to use a chair all the time. He wanted to do more things without help.

Playing basketball showed him the wheelchair was nothing more than a tool. It didn't say anything about him except he needed that tool to move. It didn't say he wasn't smart. It didn't say he wasn't funny. It didn't say anything about him. It was no different than someone wearing glasses.

"Peter, you up?" his mom called.

"Yeah, Mom," he answered as he scooted out of bed. *Enough thinking about it. Time to face it* he said to himself.

As he rolled into the van and locked himself in, he thought again how lucky he was that his mom was home. The school had offered a bus to get him to school and back. It had a lift, like an outside elevator that would lift him in his chair into the bus. But for some reason, that made him feel less capable. With the van, he could wheel himself in and lock himself in place. Now that he understood there were tools that let him do things himself, that's all he wanted. He wanted to do everything by himself that he could while he could. *Someday that would change, but not today*, he thought as they pulled up to school.

Mr. S was outside waiting when his mom pulled into the accessible parking spot. His real name was Mr. Stevenson, but everyone called him Mr. S. He was the teacher who made sure Peter had what he needed to learn despite his mitochondrial disease. Mr. S had a great sense of humor and they had a lot of fun together. Not every year at school had been a good one. But this year was amazing. Mr. S was the best and he really liked his classroom teacher, Mrs. Erickson. They both loved to laugh and didn't get upset if he had a bad day.

Mito made his energy level vary from day to day. On a really bad day, he only had the mental energy to pick options instead of think of the answers himself. So those days, Mr. S gave him multiple choice answers to pick from. Thankfully, those days were pretty rare. Most of the time, he could think of his own answers. Math was easiest for him; reading was often the hardest. He loved making up stories, but Mr. S usually did the actual writing. Peter was starting to use a computer to write, but it still took him a really long time to find the letters. He did love the *Type to Learn* game he played at school. He was getting better.

Mr. S walked alongside as Peter rolled himself down the hall. Despite the kids looking at him, he couldn't help but grin. He was doing it himself. No wall to hold, no leaning on anyone else. With his backpack on the back of the chair, he was his own man!

Justin and Sean came up to him as they entered the classroom. They immediately started talking about the Philadelphia Eagles win the day before. Mr. S gave him the backpack and Peter was able to unpack his homework and put everything in his desk. He rolled over to the cubbies and hung the backpack on his assigned hook. It was a little challenging to wheel around the desks and chairs, but he figured that would be good practice for moving around the basketball court and other players. Mrs. Erickson had moved his desk to the corner of the room. He was near the door, close to the cubbies, and not far from the reading table. As he rolled back and tucked his chair under his desk, he grinned. *I got this!* he thought.

The day passed quickly. He was allowed to leave class a few minutes early for lunch, recess, and related arts. That way he could get to where he needed to be before the halls were crowded with other kids. At lunch, Mr. S told him he could roll his chair up to the end of the cafeteria table. It was perfect. Justin sat on one end and Sean on the other. Philadelphia had made it into the playoffs and they spent all of lunch predicting what that weekend's game would be like and who they'd play in the Super Bowl.

"At recess, we all played basketball! That was the best," Peter told his mom at dinner that night. "I didn't need help. I didn't have to worry about losing my balance. I could chase the balls just like them, *and* I didn't shoot any air balls!"

"It was especially sweet," he told his dad over bites of chicken, "when Tim walked by. He had nothing to say!"

"What do you mean?" his dad asked.

"Well, in reading today, I kept getting stuck on the word *charged*. We were reading about magnets and I kept forgetting to flip the g to the j sound. Tim made some crack about my reading. But I just looked at him and said, 'Well I might not be that good at reading, but you should see me play basketball!' Then Mrs. Erickson jumped in and told us both to stop arguing.

At recess, he came over while we were playing ball. I think he was just about to say something, but then Sean passed the ball to Justin at the three-point line. I was rolling toward the basket so Justin bounce-passed it to me. I caught it and made the layup as I rolled under the net. It was a totally sweet play! And Tim just turned around and walked away."

"Way to go, Champ!" Dad said as we high-fived.

"I'm so glad you had a good day, honey," Peter's mom chimed in. "Sounds like you enjoyed using the chair at school?"

"I'm so glad we got it, Mom," Peter replied. "I know some kids were staring today, but they'll get used to it just like they did with my walker. The best part is how much I can do by myself. I can just roll over to where I need to be – no more having Mr. S bring my walker to my desk and help me up. With the walker, the grown-ups were always worrying about me falling over. People were always hovering around me. Now, I'm just like everyone else.

But there's still one problem with my chair."

"What's that?" his mom asked.

"I still need those flames on the side," he said as they all laughed.

Chapter 7

Peter pulled on his Easton Eagles shirt and headed downstairs for breakfast. If only it was in Philadelphia's green and black it would be perfect, he thought. He loved the phrase, Fly Like an Eagle, on the back. That's what life felt like again. Free. He could fly like an eagle all by himself in his chair. And that's what I'm going to do today, he told himself. We are going to win this tournament!

"Ready for the big day?" his mom asked as she set down some scrambled eggs and toast in front of him.

"Yep," he replied. "We're going to win the whole thing today!"

"Well, you guys did look really good yesterday. But remember, winning isn't as important as playing well."

"But it sure feels good," Peter said laughing. "I know, Mom. I messed up a few times yesterday. I didn't realize Kolby wasn't looking when I passed her the ball that one time and it went out of bounds. I also didn't get back on defense fast enough and the Pittsburg player went right in with a layup. That almost cost us the game, if it hadn't been for Juan's basket and free throw at the buzzer."

"Don't just focus on the mistakes though, Peter. It's important to learn from them, yes. But you really played well yesterday," his Dad joined in. "You'd never know this was your first season. You've gotten stronger. Most of your passes were right on target yesterday. You're like a brick wall on defense. And you listened well to Coach Jenny as she called out plays and made adjustments. What's most important is that you play as a team and do your best."

"Can we go now?" Peter asked as he shoved the last bite of toast in his mouth.

— — —

The parking lot was crowded as they pulled in. Three other teams from nearby states had come into town for the weekend tournament. They had games for the 7-9 year olds, Peter's group, the Prep teams, and the Varsity high schoolers. They used the side baskets for the younger groups so two games could happen at the same time. But the high schoolers played full-court games. Games happened all day Saturday and today were the three championship games.

Today they would play the Virginia Tigers. Peter's game wasn't until after lunch, but there were still two varsity-level games this morning. Their games took longer with two 20-minute halves. They played full court with the 10-foot baskets so they couldn't have more than one game at a time. He wanted to watch them play.

Someday, I'll do that, Peter thought as he watched the Easton players warming up. Kevin had made a three-point shot, nothing but net. When Peter first started playing, he could barely get the ball to the 8 ½ foot rim, used at his level. But now, he could. A few more years, and he'd move to the 10-foot once he reached high school. Peter grinned thinking back to how just a few months ago he didn't even know wheelchair basketball existed. Now he couldn't imagine life without it.

Finally, it was time for the game. Coach Jenny had all eight of them do five laps from the base line to mid-court and back to get warmed up. Then she ran them through some stretches.

"Scissor your arms straight, cross in front, then back out wide. Switch- right cross on top, then next time left arm, and repeat. Good, now arms over your head and down by your sides. Keep going, Juan. Get yourself warmed up. Punch out now, straight ahead, right punch, left punch.

Now swing your arms together side to side. Twist at the middle. Nice work everyone.

Final stretches. Put your left hand on your right elbow and pull that arm across your body. Count to 10. Now put the right hand behind your head and push that elbow back to stretch that tricep. Count to 10. Good, now repeat on the left side."

When the ref walked over to say they were ready to start, Coach Jenny called everyone into the circle. "Alright gang, we know what to do. Think about what we've been practicing. Look for open passes as you move down on offense. Get back quick on defense. Play smart and safe. Most importantly, have fun!" she said grinning. "Hands in, Eagles on three."

"One, two, three… Eagles!" everyone yelled.

Their game had four eight-minute quarters. Peter didn't get to start but he knew he'd get to play soon. He cheered from the sidelines. The team looked great and soon they were ahead 10 to 6.

"Jackie, Drew, out. DeVonte, Peter in," Coach Jenny called.

Juan had just scored again so the boys joined in and set up on defense. Peter and Juan set up back to back at the top of the key. As the Tigers brought the ball down, they each picked up a player. Peter kept his chair between the player and the basket, forcing him to stay wide of the lane. Juan's player passed him the ball and Peter's hands shot up to block it. The player still managed to catch it but struggled to see around Peter's arms. DeVonte's player moved out from under the basket, ready for a pass. Peter saw him and when his player passed the ball, Peter knocked it off course. It bounced off DeVonte's player's chair and rolled out of bounds.

Our ball, Peter thought and he headed down the court.

"Stay out wide," Peter heard Coach Jenny call. "Not too far, Peter. Who can she pass too? Look at the ball, everyone."

Kolby passed the ball to Juan. He tried to get a shot but the Tigers filled the lane. He passed it back to Kolby and she passed it to Peter. Two fast passes caught the Tigers off guard. Peter saw DeVonte was open and bounce-passed it to him. He got the shot off but the Tiger on defense got the rebound.

Missed shot, they have the rebound, Peter thought. *Get back on defense. Where's the ball? Get over there. Block him! Hands up. Go for the ball*, Peter coached himself.

Back and forth, the game went on. They were up by ten in the third quarter and Peter was back in the game. He was glad he'd had a chance to rest. His arms were getting tired. But he wanted to be in. He wanted to play.

Easton
Easton

Juan brought the ball down the court after the Tiger's last missed shot. Peter rolled down right. He went low by the basket this time instead of staying near the foul line like normal. He wanted to throw off the Tiger guarding him. Grabbing his left wheel with his hand, he spun his chair around and moved back toward the top of the key. Juan saw he was open and passed him the ball. But Peter hadn't fully finished the turn so he didn't get his hands up in time. The ball hit him full in the face.

"Time!" called the ref. Coach Jenny came running out on the court.

"Peter, are you okay?" she asked.

Peter's face was stinging. "Ow! Man that hurt," he cried. "Yeah, I'm okay," he said, blinking his eyes and shaking his head.

Juan rolled up, "Sorry Peter. I didn't mean to do that. You okay?"

"Yeah, I'm okay. Guess that's one way to catch a pass," he laughed.

Coach Jenny had Jackie go back into the game while Peter took a quick break on the sidelines. His mom came rushing up. "Ow, Peter. Are you okay?" She brushed his hair out of his eyes, noticing the red welt on his cheek where the ball had hit.

"I'm fine, Mom!" Peter replied. "It was just a ball. Coach, can I go back in the game?"

Coach Jenny looked at his mom and smiled. "You've got one tough cookie there, Ms. Thomas. He's okay. Missed his nose thankfully. Sure Peter, next break."

Back in the game, Peter focused on defense. It was still hard to make a basket but he knew he could help the team by keeping the Tigers from scoring.

"Stay on your player," he heard Coach Jenny call. The player he was guarding caught the ball and looked for a shot. Peter had his chair between the player and the basket, his hands in the Tiger's face. When he lowered the ball looking to pass instead, Peter reached out and knocked the ball loose. It rolled down the court toward their basket. Kolby took off from the top of the key. As she caught up to the ball she rolled beside it. Holding the ball against the wheel, it rolled up into her arms just in time for her to make the layup.

"Great shot, Kolby. Nice steal, Peter," Coach Jenny called from the sidelines. Kolby gave him a high five as they set up again on defense.

Soon the game had just a few minutes left and Peter knew Coach Jenny would put in other players soon. He secretly wished he could make a shot. That would make today perfect.

Kolby was bringing the ball down. Juan went wide on the left side of the key. Peter went to the right but saw that DeVonte had been kept wide by one of the Tiger defenders. Peter had a clear path to the basket. Juan saw it too.

"He's open, pass the ball," Juan yelled to Kolby. She passed it to Juan who bounced it to Peter as he rolled up to the basket. It was a perfect pass. Right into his lap like the coaches did at practice. Two feet from the basket Peter got his wish. He lined up the ball with the corner of the backstop and made the shot!

"Whooohoo!" Peter yelled.

Finally! Points in a game, he thought as he and Juan high-fived!

Chapter 8

"So wheelchair basketball season is over? Are you going to try some other sports at Easton?" Justin asked.

He and Peter were heading into the gym. There was an assembly for the whole school. Mrs. Erickson had sent them in early to get Peter settled. Since Peter couldn't sit up in the bleachers with the rest of the class, she let Justin sit down with him on the first row.

"I'm definitely going to try other sports. Coach Jenny thinks she can teach me to swim. I want to try wheelchair baseball and tennis. My Dad played tennis in high school. But I'm really excited about track. Coach Mike showed me a race runner last week. It's like a giant three-wheeled bike but it doesn't have any pedals. You run with it instead. I could run again Justin!"

"Wow! I didn't realize there were so many kinds of adaptive sports," Justin replied.

"I know," Peter said. "It's a whole new world."

The boys kept chatting while the classes filed in. "Do you know what this assembly is about?" Justin asked.

"Mrs. Erickson said it's called DAP day – it stands for Disability Awareness Program," Peter answered. "I don't know any more than that."

Pretty soon, Principal Jackson got on the mic and called everyone to attention.

"Welcome Greenspring Elementary! Clap your hands if you are having a great day!"

All the kids clapped like crazy until she signaled for quiet. "Today we have a real treat for you. How many of you have ever needed help before?" she asked.

Everyone responded with a raised hand.

"That's right! We all need help at some time or another. The issue isn't about whether we need help or not, but about how and when we need help. Some people need extra help from a teacher to learn reading or math. Some people need help from glasses to help them see. Some people need equipment to help them walk or move."

Peter noticed one of the first graders looking at him when Principal Jackson said that.

"What are you looking at?" Justin said, looking at the boy. The boy quickly turned around and faced the principal. Peter smiled.

"Today you get the chance to meet some amazing people who didn't let needing help stop them from doing what they wanted to do. Please help me welcome our special guests with the Disability Awareness Program."

Everyone clapped and cheered as five people, dressed as athletes, came into the gym. Peter broke into a grin when he saw the first woman enter in her wheelchair. Behind her, three men and one more woman rolled in. Some were in sports chairs like Peter used at Easton. One of the men was in a racing chair Peter knew was used for track races and marathons. Another man was in a recumbent handcycle. It allowed him to lie down and crank the pedals with his hands to make it move.

All of the kids started talking at once, pointing at the different people and their chairs. The five athletes did a lap around the gym. It was everything Peter could do to not roll out there and join them. Finally, they lined up in the middle of the gym and faced the bleachers.

The woman who had rolled in first introduced the other athletes. She explained why each person was in a wheelchair. One had had cancer when she was a baby. The treatment had cured her of cancer but caused other challenges that left her with limited ability to walk. The kids went crazy when she got out of her wheelchair and started using crutches instead.

One of the men had been in a motorcycle accident. He had a spinal cord injury that left him paralyzed from the waist down. Another man had been in the military. He was injured fighting overseas and now his left leg had nothing below the knee. When he got out of his chair and put on a prosthetic, the kids started up again, talking and pointing. The other man had a disease that made his bones very brittle. It was safer for him to be in a chair than risk falling down.

I can relate to that, Peter thought.

Finally, the speaker introduced herself as Ms. Kate. She explained she had been born with spina bifida. Her spine and spinal cord had not developed right before she was born.

"That's what Juan has," Peter whispered to Justin.

"As you can see," Ms. Kate continued, "there are many, many ways people can become disabled. To be disabled simply means a part or parts of one's body doesn't work as it should. People used to make fun of disabled people. They thought they weren't smart and couldn't live a normal life. Some countries around the world still reject children who are born with a disability. But our program is working to change that. Today, we want to show you there's almost nothing we can't do!"

The kids cheered as one of the women and men wheeled in a cart loaded with sports equipment. Over the next 30 minutes, the athletes demonstrated how to use different adaptive equipment to play various sports. They had a sled used in sled hockey. They modeled and explained how wheelchair tennis, baseball, softball, and lacrosse were played. They explained adaptive soccer, racing, volleyball, bocci and curling. They talked about other adaptive sports like archery, sailing, rugby, motocross, and bowling too. Even Peter was impressed… and he'd seen the Eagles athletes in action.

"Being disabled no longer means you can't do things. It just means you need to find a new way to do it. Sometimes that means special equipment. Sometimes it means a new technique. But what it doesn't mean is you have to quit and give up!" Ms. Kate explained. "We all face challenges in life. You might be able to walk like I can't, but I know you have challenges in your life. Every person does. But just like us, all that means is you need to find the right tool to help you do it. You can overcome anything," she continued.

"For our final activity, we thought we should play some basketball! What do you say?"

The students roared. The man with the prosthetic pulled three kid-size sports chairs off the trailer. "Who wants to play?" he yelled.

Every student jumped to their feet, calling "Me! Me!" and raising their hand.

Ms. Kate wheeled over to Peter.

"Hi Peter!"

Peter couldn't believe she knew his name!

"I hear you've become quite a basketball player this year. Want to show us what you got?"

"You bet!" Peter grinned and rolled onto the court. Mr. S came up and waited for Peter to switch into one of the chairs. Then he rolled Peter's wheelchair back to the sideline by Justin.

A fifth-grade girl was chosen to play, and then they picked Tim.

Tim! Oh no! Peter thought to himself. But he couldn't stay upset long. Soon the game began and he was flying like an eagle.

Three of the adults were on one team. The kids were on the other. But the other two adults, Ms. Kate and the man with the prosthetic joined their team and coached the kids along. Soon they left Peter alone, recognizing he knew what he was doing. Ms. Kate had to help Tim a lot. He had trouble coordinating his pushing and kept leaning forward. Peter chuckled to himself. *Been there, done that,* he thought.

The adults kept stealing the ball and making trick shots. This is like playing with the Globe Trotters, Peter told the 5th grader. Determined to play seriously, he got in a position to play defense. He made sure he kept his chair between the player and the net. When his player got the ball, he started teasing Peter, holding the ball out to see if he wanted it.

Big mistake, Peter thought. He hit the ball hard and knocked it out of the man's hand. Then he took off after the ball, leaving the surprised man still sitting there. Ms. Kate fielded the ball as Peter reached midcourt. She bounce-passed it to Peter. He caught the ball and tucked it under his chin as he pushed his chair twice. Then he bounced the ball out in front of him and rolled up under it to catch it. He steered his chair to the right side of the key. With one more push, he picked up the ball, lined up with the corner of the square on the backboard and shot the ball.

"Yes!" he screamed. He made the shot. He made a 10-foot basket! The kids were screaming too.

Tim rolled up beside him. "Wow, Peter! Great shot!"

"Thanks, Tim," Peter grinned. "Isn't this awesome?"

"Awesome? This is hard! I don't know how you do it! I can't even get my chair going the way I want it to. Hey, I'm really sorry I've been messing with you. You seemed to get all the attention from everyone. I never realized how hard things must be. I screwed up, Peter. I'm really sorry," Tim said. "Do you think maybe sometime I can join you guys at recess and play some basketball?"

Peter tried to get the shocked look off his face. "Hey man, no big deal right? Recess sounds great. For now, let's go play some right now."

He grabbed his left wheel and spun his chair around. "Time to fly," he called as he headed back into the game.

What are Adaptive Sports?

Adaptive sports is the term used to describe sports modified in a way that allows people with physical, and sometimes mental, disabilities to participate. Often this involves specialized equipment such as a wheelchair or a prosthetic. Sports for athletes with visual disabilities might use a ball with bells inside so the athlete can hear it, or runners who are blind have a guide that runs with them. Most sports try to maintain the same rules as the non-adaptive version. But sometimes a few rules might need to be adjusted. For example, the primary difference between wheelchair and standing basketball involves dribbling. Wheelchair athletes must pass or bounce the ball after two pushes of their wheelchair to avoid a traveling violation.

Many adaptive sports were created by soldiers after World War II as part of their rehabilitation that was then maintained for recreation and eventually competition. Wheelchair basketball is one such sport that was developed by soldiers injured in WWII. It became one of the original eight sports at the first Paralympics in Rome in 1960. The other sports were archery, Para athletics (track & field events), dartchery (a sport combining darts and archery), snooker (similar to pool or billiards), Para swimming, table tennis, and wheelchair fencing.

The Paralympics are the culminating event for athletes with physical disabilities. Athletes with mental disabilities compete in the Special Olympics. But adaptive sports is not just about Olympic competition. Just like sports are an everyday occurrence for children without disabilities, whether at recess, in the neighborhood, or on an organized team, adaptive sports need to be a part of everyday life for children with disabilities too. Whether joining in at recess, being included in gym class or PE, or playing with other children on your street, all children need the benefits of exercise, teamwork, and belonging. Having a disability might mean one can't play the same as others, but it does not mean one can't play! You simply have to find the right equipment, and/or the right sport. Thankfully many, many options are available. Use the following resources to find an option that works for you!

Listing of Adaptive Sports Programs throughout the United States:

https://www.challengedathletes.org/adaptive-sport-organizations/

American Association of AdaptED Sports Programs: https://adaptedsports.org/

AAASP's mission is to expand and sustain a standardized structure for education-based athletic competition to improve the well-being of students with physical disabilities.

Move United: https://moveunitedsport.org/

Nationwide organization to ensure all children through age 12 have access to 70 different sports with 244 community member organizations in 45 states.

Wheelchair Sports Federation:

https://wheelchairsportsfederation.org/

US Paralympics Team:

https://www.usopc.org/paralympic-sport-development

Special Olympics: https://www.specialolympics.org/

How Does Wheelchair Basketball Compare to Standing Basketball?

Wheelchair basketball was developed by soldiers after World War II around 1946. It is one of the oldest adaptive sports and was one of the original sports included in the first Paralympics.

As with most adaptive sports, the goal is to keep the adaptive version as close to the standing version as possible. The court size, basketball, scoring, and most rules are the same in wheelchair basketball as in standing basketball. Games may have four periods of 10 minutes or two halves of 20 minutes.

The biggest difference between standing basketball and wheelchair basketball is in dribbling. To dribble in wheelchair basketball, the ball can be held on a player's lap for two pushes before the player must bounce the ball on the floor, or pass or shoot. To take a third push would be considered traveling. Thus, there is no double dribbling in wheelchair basketball.

When shooting free throws, only the rear wheels must be behind the line, keeping the distance more equal to standing basketball.

With younger players or beginners, modifications can be made to accommodate the varying abilities. Prep or Junior teams might adjust the court size, length of games or equipment. For example, an 8.5-foot basket or a smaller ball such as a woman's or rookie ball are common modifications used.

National Wheelchair Basketball Association:

https://www.nwba.org/

Move United Wheelchair Basketball Resource:

https://moveunitedsport.org/app/uploads/2021/07/Wheelchair-Basketball_PRINT-1-1.pdf

Move United: https://moveunitedsport.org/sport/basketball/

Challenged Athletes Foundation:

https://www.challengedathletes.org/training-zone/

What is Mitochondrial Disease?

Every part of your body is made up of very tiny things called cells. On average there are around 37 trillion cells in a grown person. That's 37,000,000,000,000 cells! You need a microscope to see a cell. In fact, they are so small, that thousands of cells would fit inside the period at the end of this sentence. That's tiny!

The cells are designed to do all the different jobs our body needs. There are skin cells, blood cells, hair cells, muscle cells, brain cells, stomach cells… all the different kinds needed for a body to work. Inside most of these cells, there's an oval-shaped piece called the mitochondria. It has several jobs, but the main job is to make energy. Each cell needs energy to do the job it was made for. The mitochondria use the food and oxygen we eat and breathe to make that energy.

Someone with mitochondrial disease has a problem in the mitochondria. It can't make energy the right way. This is not a disease you can catch, like a cold or the flu. It must be inherited from your parents, or their parents, or someone in the family history - the same way you get your eye color, the color of your hair, and how tall you will be.

Because so many different kinds of cells exist, there are many different kinds of mitochondrial disease. Body parts that need the most energy are usually most affected. Those are your brain, nerves, muscles, heart, pancreas, liver, kidneys, eyes and ears. Often several of these body parts will have problems depending on what type of mitochondrial disease the person has. The United Mitochondrial Disease Foundation (UMDF) lists 47 broad types of mito disease on its website, many with the same symptoms. But there are hundreds of variations, just like there are many kinds of cancer. It is estimated that 1 in 5000 people are born with a genetic mitochondrial disease.

My son, upon whom Peter in this story is based, had PolG. It mainly affected his muscles, brain, liver, eyesight and digestion. Peter's symptoms started after he turned four. We worked with doctors to manage his symptoms and not make his body need more energy than it could create.

Like my son, Peter, many people with mito disease take specific vitamins and supplements that can help the body struggle less with making energy. But it does not fix the problem. So far, individuals with mitochondrial disorders have no cure for their disease. The younger a person is when symptoms start, the shorter their life will likely be.

Scientists who study the mitochondria have made steady progress in identifying the diseases caused by mitochondrial dysfunction and in managing the symptoms or effects of the disease to slow down its progress. But more research is needed to find a cure.

Check out these resources for more information about Mitochondrial disease:

United Mitochondrial Disease Foundation-

https://www.umdf.org/

Phone: 412-793-8077 or 888-317-8633

MitoAction- https://www.mitoaction.org/

Phone: 888-648-6228

Cleveland Clinic-

https://my.clevelandclinic.org/health/diseases/15612-mitochondrial-diseases

National Organization for Rare Disorders (NORD)-

https://rarediseases.org/

Phone: 203-744-0100

Genetic and Rare Diseases (GARD) Information Center-

https://rarediseases.info.nih.gov/